When to Trust Your Gut? The Effectiveness of Intuition in Organizational Decision-Making

Sabina Dörner

Bibliographic information published by the German National Library:

The German National Library lists this publication in the National Bibliography; detailed bibliographic data are available on the Internet at http://dnb.dnb.de.

ISBN: 9783346608093
This book is also available as an ebook.

© GRIN Publishing GmbH
Nymphenburger Straße 86
80636 München

Print and binding: Books on Demand GmbH, Norderstedt, Germany
Printed on acid-free paper from responsible sources.

The present work has been carefully prepared. Nevertheless, authors and publishers do not incur liability for the correctness of information, notes, links and advice as well as any printing errors.

GRIN web shop: https://www.grin.com/document/1184297

When to Trust Your Gut? The Effectiveness of Intuition

in Organizational Decision-Making

Maastricht University

School of Business and Economics

Dörner, S.

SBE Pre-Master

Organisational Behaviour

1 April 2021

Literature Review

Table of Contents

1. Introduction

Decision-making plays a crucial role in the organization's success (Ceschi et al., 2017). Ceschi et al. (2017) establish that making high-quality and efficient decisions is a key competence of high-performing organizations. The last two decades have seen major changes in organizational structures and processes due to technological advances and societal developments (Ackerman & Kanfer, 2020; Barley et al., 2017). Accordingly, the circumstances in which decisions are made have changed and become more challenging (Ackerman & Kanfer, 2020; Barley et al., 2017). As Sadler-Smith and Shefy (2004) point out, organizational decisions can involve a large amount of information to be processed. This increases the complexity of decision-making processes. Time is also often limited, and decisions must be made under fast-moving conditions (Sadler-Smith & Shefy, 2004). Furthermore, Faraji-Rad and Pham (2017) suggest that the database of information available can be inadequate or ambiguous, which makes the decision's outcome difficult to predict. Organizational decisions can hence be associated with a high degree of uncertainty (Faraji-Rad & Pham, 2017). Traditionally, organizations aim for a rational approach to decision-making. To decide rationally, all relevant information must be considered (Sadler-Smith & Shefy, 2004). However, according to the authors, changing working conditions require individuals to make decisions quickly and in uncertain situations. Under such conditions, a rational model to decision-making cannot be applied because the human capacity to process information is limited (Halevy & Chou, 2014). Consequently, individuals must rely on their intuition. Decisions in an organizational context are therefore often taken not only in a rational way but also by intuition (Faraji-Rad & Pham, 2017; Sadler-Smith & Shefy, 2004). As empirical findings confirm, 47% of employees often decide intuitively (Tichá et al., 2010).

Previous research indicates that intuitive decision-making yields creative and original outcomes (Dane et al., 2012). Several studies demonstrate that individuals who trust their intuition generate innovative ideas and solutions to problems (Garfield et al., 2001; Zhu et al., 2017). Similarly, Eubanks et al. (2010) conclude that these decisions are of higher quality and utility. While these empirical studies collectively suggest that using intuition improves decision-making effectiveness, it is also prone to bias and can result in errors and misleading judgments (Sadler-Smith & Shefy, 2004).

In organizations, there is growing pressure to make decisions both quickly and effectively (Perlow et al., 2002). Dane and Pratt (2007) propose that the use of intuition is effective to make decisions within a short time. Consequently, it is crucial to understand what influences intuitive decision-making and its effectiveness. Therefore, this paper investigates the factors that determine whether or not the use of intuition is effective in decision-making. This paper aims to examine whether organizations benefit in the long term when their employees make decisions intuitively rather than rationally. From this, implications for managers on how to effectively make intuitive decisions in organizations are derived.

This paper begins by defining and conceptualizing intuitive decision-making and discussing its benefits and limitations in an organizational context. Then, it elaborates on intuitive decision-making effectiveness and analyzes the key factors that determine the effectiveness. Finally, this paper presents evidence-based advice for managers on how to implement and foster effective intuitive decision-making in organizations.

2. Literature Review

The following section provides definitions and approaches to conceptualizing intuition in decision-making. It then places intuitive decision-making in the organizational context and explains its benefits and limitations. Furthermore, this part of the paper investigates the factors that influence effectiveness.

2.1 Intuitive Decision-Making

Intuitive decision-making can be defined as the unconscious processing of information that results in direct knowing without conscious inference (Sinclair & Ashkanasy, 2005). Likewise, Eubanks et al. (2010) explain that intuition entails the ability to know without objective analysis or logical reasoning. In addition, Dane and Pratt (2007) describe intuitive decision-making as the recognition of patterns that lead to affective arguments. This happens quickly and unconsciously (Dane & Pratt, 2007). Based on these characteristics, intuition can be distinguished from the rational approach to making decisions (Dane et al., 2012). In contrast, rational decision-making implies conscious, deliberative, and analytical thinking (Sadler-Smith & Shefy, 2004).

The phenomenon of intuition in decision-making is further conceptualized by Miller and Ireland (2005). They use two different approaches: Intuition as a holistic hunch and as automated expertise. Similarly, Sadler-Smith and Shefy (2004) point out, that intuition can be conceived as knowledge, based on expertise, and as sensation, based on feelings (Sadler-Smith & Shefy, 2004). Intuition as a holistic hunch or as sensation refers to decisions made in response to information that has been unconsciously synthesized from experiences (Miller & Ireland, 2005). Dane and Pratt (2007) argue that experiences from past situations are summarized as unconscious cognitive patterns. When faced with a decision, individuals unconsciously draw holistic associations to these patterns and make judgments (Dane & Pratt, 2007). According to Mille and Ireland (2005), intuition as automated expertise or as knowledge is based on a sense of familiarity. When a decision has been made similarly before, previously acquired knowledge related to this situation is applied. Thus, the decision is made through a subconscious process involving past learning and the recognition of patterns (Miller & Ireland, 2005). Automated expertise develops over time as it is the accumulation of extensive experiences in particular fields (Salas et al., 2010). Intuitive decisions are hence taken unconsciously based on patterns of information and situation-specific expertise (Dane & Pratt, 2007; Miller & Ireland, 2005; Salas et al., 2010).

Rational decision-making is still the preferred approach in today's organizations (Robbins & Judge, 2019). This is due to the prevailing assumption that rational decisions are value-maximizing, efficient, and less biased than intuitive decisions (Sadler-Smith & Shefy, 2004). However, Sadler-Smith and Shefy (2004) point out that decisions are based on both intuition and rational analysis. Consequently, the authors argue that using intuition is as important as using rationality (Sadler-Smith & Shefy, 2004). Likewise, Elbanna (2006) notes that intuitive decisions in organizations are becoming more common due to increasingly ambiguous, and time-limited work conditions. This view is supported by empirically collected data which suggest that managers rely extensively on their intuition when making decisions (Burke & Miller, 1999).

Consistent with the preference for rationality in decision-making is the widely held assumption that rational processes yield better outcomes than intuitive processes (Elbanna, 2006). However, existing literature indicates that intuitive decision-making has multiple benefits (Dane et al., 2012). Previous research establishes that intuitive decisions are of higher creativity (Zhu et al., 2017) and higher originality (Garfield et al., 2001) than deliberative decisions. Similarly, Eubanks et al. (2010) find that intuitive individuals generate more creative ideas and problem solutions. Furthermore, these ideas are more qualitative and useful (Eubanks et al., 2010). In the same vein, Huang and Pearce (2015) conclude that individuals decide intuitively when they aim for original and feasible outcomes. Moreover, multiple researchers investigate intuitive decision-making in different situations. For instance, using intuition is particularly effective in detecting deception (Albrechtsen et al., 2009) and in complex circumstances (Usher et al., 2011). Another benefit of using intuition is that individuals can evaluate decisions more accurately because they are not overly focused on the potential risks (Zhu et al., 2017). In addition, Burke and Miller (1999) show that intuition speeds up the process of decision-making, enhances flexibility, and enables adaptation to changing environments. The researchers also document improved decision outcomes, such as higher product quality and increased customer satisfaction. Additionally, intuitively based decisions tend to be consistent with the company's culture and values (Burke & Miller, 1999). Together, the studies presented provide evidence that the use of intuition in decision-making can be beneficial and enhance the decision's effectiveness.

However, intuitive decision-making is also subject to criticism. As Sadler-Smith and Shefy (2004) argue, individuals apply heuristics in the decision-making process when using their intuition. These can lead to errors and biases in judgments (Sadler-Smith & Shefy, 2004). Sauter (1999) also questions the effectiveness of intuitive decisions. He claims that the use of intuition increases the tendency to ignore relevant details and facts (Sauter, 1999). Though existing literature suggests that intuition can be prone to bias, it provides many benefits and opportunities for improving decision-making in organizations (Dane et al., 2012).

2.2 Factors Influencing the Effectiveness of Intuitive Decision-Making

As established in the previous section, deciding intuitively is a valuable skill in organizational decision-making (Dane et al., 2012). To use intuition effectively, it is important to understand what impacts the effectiveness of intuitive decision-making (Salas et al., 2010). In this respect, previous research points to several influential factors: the decision-maker, the decision task, and the decision environment (Salas et al., 2010).

As previously discussed, intuition is based on the recognition of patterns through experience with similar situations (Miller & Ireland, 2005). According to Salas et al. (2010), experience within a particular field develops into an expertise over time. Consequently, expertise enhances the effectiveness of intuition in decision-making (Salas et al., 2010). As a decision maker's level of experience and knowledge increases, so does the number of familiar patterns that the individual possesses (Matzler et al., 2007). Intuition thus improves because there are more cognitive patterns that the decision-maker can intuitively recognize (Matzler et al., 2007). Moreover, Salas et al. (2010) suggest that a knowledge base that exceeds explicit knowledge and implies implicit learning is most beneficial to decision-makers (Salas et al., 2010). This view is supported by evidence of one study in a clinical setting (Nyatanga & Vocht, 2008) and two laboratory studies (Dane et al., 2012). However, the effect of expertise is limited to the domain in which knowledge was acquired. When expertise is used in a different context, intuitive decision-making may be less effective (Dane & Pratt, 2007).

To develop an expertise-based intuition, obtaining feedback is equally important as gaining experience (Salas et al., 2010). Salas et al. (2010) conclude that feedback is essential for implicit learning, from which expertise evolves. Accordingly, receiving feedback enhances the development of accurate intuitions and improves decision-making skills (Sadler-Smith & Shefy, 2004). Therefore, the effectiveness of intuitive decisions increases with the availability of feedback (Salas et al., 2010).

Another factor influencing the effectiveness of intuition is the decision maker's personality (Salas et al., 2010). As Mick (2014) notes, some individuals are by nature more intuitive due to certain personality traits. Likewise, Salas et al. (2010) identify a tendency of individuals to rely on either intuitive or deliberate processing. Burke and Miller's (1999) study shows that intuitive managers are perceived as confident, open-minded, reflective, and flexible in their thinking and actions. They are also associated with a high willingness to take risks, fairness, empathy, and creativity (Burke & Miller, 1999). In addition, emotional intelligence is also considered a characteristic of intuitive individuals, as they can recognize and interpret their intuitive feelings (Matzler et al., 2007).

Regarding the decision task, the task type and structure are significant factors (Salas et al., 2010). As noted by Dane and Pratt (2007), the effectiveness of the use of intuition depends on whether the task is more intellectual or judgmental. Intellectual tasks can be decomposed into a sequence of operations while judgmental tasks cannot be solved sequentially using logical steps, such as evaluating the morality of behavior (Dane et al., 2012). Intuition is likely to be effective in tasks of judgmental nature because intuitive processing enables the integration of elements of non-decomposable tasks through holistic associations (Dane & Pratt, 2007; Dane et al., 2012). In addition, existing literature indicates that task complexity impacts the intuition's effectiveness (Dane & Pratt, 2007; Dijksterhuis et al., 2006). As previously noted, Dane and Pratt (2007) argue that intuitive reasoning, in contrast to deliberate reasoning, integrates a large amount of information by synthesizing complex elements. Therefore, intuitive decision-making is more effective for tasks of high complexity (Dane & Pratt, 2007). Complex tasks, for instance, involve multiple possible solutions and do not have a definite success criterion (Dane & Pratt, 2007). Similarly, Dijksterhuis et al. (2006) show that complex decisions are made most effectively through intuition. However, another study finds a preference for choosing an intuitive decision-making style when tasks have a simple rather than complex structure (Inbar et al., 2010). Taken all evidence presented together, intuitive decision-making is most beneficial when a task is judgmental, non-decomposable, and complex (Salas et al., 2010).

Furthermore, the environment in which an organization operates also determines the effectiveness of intuitive decision-making (Salas et al., 2010). Kahneman and Klein (2009) identify two environmental factors that must be present for effective intuitive decisions. Firstly, the environment must have a sufficiently regulated structure and provide valid cues (Kahneman & Klein, 2009). These cues are available and specific information regarding a situation, such as obvious symptoms of a disease. Secondly, the environment must provide opportunities to apply the cues and practice intuition (Kahneman & Klein, 2009). In the same vein, Khatri and Ng (2000) distinguish the environment by the degree of its stability. Environmental instability is shaped by time pressures, a large amount of information to be processed, and lacking certainty regarding this information. In unstable environments, the use of intuition most likely leads to effective decisions (Khatri & Ng, 2000). In addition, a tolerant environment that allows both positive and negative learnings fosters intuitive decision-making with high effectiveness (Matzler et al., 2007). Likewise, effectiveness depends on whether the environment provides opportunities to make new experiences (Matzler et al., 2017). Overall, intuitive decision-makers benefit from environments that provide valuable information, opportunities for learning and exploration, and are unstable and tolerant (Khatri & Ng, 2000; Kahneman & Klein, 2009; Matzler et al., 2007).

3. Evidence-based Advice

Having discussed the relevance and effectiveness of intuition decision-making, the following section provides practical advice for managers. More precisely, this part presents interventions on how to implement and foster effective intuitive decision-making in organizations.

First, environmental conditions must be met in organizations. A work environment must be created that allows intuitive thinking (Mick, 2014). Research indicates that such an environment provides opportunities to learn and practice intuition while being tolerant of failure (Khatri & Ng, 2000; Kahneman & Klein, 2009; Matzler et al., 2007). To achieve this, managers should be willing to accept failure and not punish it. Therefore, they must value both positive and negative outcomes. Managers can create a tolerant culture by embracing risky and unconventional ideas and motivating employees to implement them. By publicly showing support for these employees, even when they fail, the management can encourage other employees to use their intuition by also taking risks (Mick, 2014). This enables employees to continuously practice their intuitive judgments by exploring options and testing new approaches.

In addition, an organization that facilitates effective intuitive decision-making must also increase curiosity in its environment (Matzler et al. 2017). Curiosity is nurtured when organizations constantly create opportunities for exploration and allow their employees to make new experiences (Matzler et al., 2017). To extend the experience of employees, managers can introduce a job rotation program. In this practice, employees regularly shift between jobs or assignments within a company (Burke & Miller, 1999). Accordingly, they are faced with numerous situations that require different approaches to decision-making. This enables learning and knowledge acquisition, thus broadening the experience in various fields. Therefore, job rotation is a means to improve intuitive judgments.

Once the conditions have been established within an organization, the second step is for managers to actively develop their employee's decision-making skills. To do this, they should take action to expand their employee's expertise and knowledge base. According to Salas et al. (2010), intuitive processing is based on expertise that results from numerous experiences. The more experienced individuals are, the more cognitive cues they can draw on to make intuitive judgments (Salas et al., 2010). Means of developing expertise are training and development programs. I recommend that managers conduct professional training that creates in-depth expertise in the respective domain. Additionally, managers should also provide exercises that apply intuitive thinking to real-life cases or hypothetical scenarios. Previous research shows that problem-solving activities in small groups enhance intuitive processing (Park & Song, 2020). Therefore, managers benefit from incorporating intuitive problem-solving exercises into training sessions. In these exercises, employees are first introduced to a real-life business problem and must imagine they already know the solution (Tesolin, 2018). They are then asked to focus on the case for several minutes and subsequently write down all possible solutions without evaluating them. Finally, small groups discuss the different perspectives and approaches to solve the business problem (Tesolin, 2018). Another method of employee development is mentoring. Managers can employ mentoring programs to develop their employee's expertise. In this practice, experts share their experiences in a particular field with a less experienced employee. This allows employees to acquire knowledge and thereby improve their intuitions.

For employees to acquire intuitive expertise, they must also receive regular feedback on their intuitive decisions. By obtaining feedback, they can improve their decision-making skills (Salas et al., 2010). Consequently, I suggest managers to integrate feedback into their daily, on-the-job communication with their employees. This feedback technique has been introduced by the company Cargill with the implementation of their "Everyday Performance Management" system (Maier, 2017). The daily feedback was positively received by the employees. 69% of the employees found it beneficial for their development and 70% felt valued by their manager (Maier, 2017). Thus, managers can adapt this feedback method to enhance the employee's decision-making.

Furthermore, managers should develop not only the expertise but also their employee's intuitive awareness (Sadler-Smith & Shefy, 2004). When employees are aware of their intuition, they can use it effectively and better reflect on their decision-making style (Hodgkinson et al., 2009). To achieve this, managers can follow the guidelines proposed by Sadler-Smith and Shefy (2004) for developing intuitive awareness. These have been incorporated into MBA programs with sustained success (Sadler-Smith & Shefy, 2007). First, employees must assess the extent to which they rely on their intuitive judgment (Sadler-Smith & Shefy, 2004). Practices such as meditation, journal writing, and mind mapping can be used to gain insight into one's intuition (Burke & Miller, 1999). To encourage employees to do these exercises, managers can create personal spaces in the organization such as niches and partially closed corners (Mick, 2014). Second, employees must practice distinguishing between instinct, insight, and intuition to develop a more accurate understanding of their intuition (Sadler-Smith & Shefy, 2004). Managers could employ workshops to do so. Third, intuitive awareness increases when valuable feedback on the employee's intuitive judgments is available (Sadler-Smith & Shefy, 2004). As previously noted, I recommend managers to integrate daily feedback in conversations with their employees. Fourth, employees must test the validity of their decisions to determine how reliable their intuition is (Sadler-Smith & Shefy, 2004). To provide opportunities for testing judgments, managers should create an organizational environment that allows failure, embraces unconventional ideas, and value positive and negative outcomes. Fifth, employees are more likely to decide intuitively when they think visually (Sadler-Smith & Shefy, 2004). Therefore, I recommend managers to make ideas and thoughts visible in the organization. To do so, they can use whiteboards, team electronic motors, and pin-up walls (Mick, 2014). Sixth, employees must recognize inconsistencies and inaccuracies in their intuitive decision-making to improve it (Sadler-Smith & Shefy, 2004). To support this, managers can conduct workshops in which employee's decisions are questioned and alternatives are developed. Last, Sadler-Smith and Shefy (2004) suggest that intuitive awareness implies that the individual recognizes and values its intuition. One approach to capturing employee's intuition is to keep a diary. In an organizational context, this can be realized through a standardized diary process that includes reflection and feedback from the manager (Sadler-Smith & Shefy, 2004).

In addition to the development of environmental conditions and decision-making skills, another way to foster intuition in organizations is to recruit highly intuitive individuals (Mick, 2014). Previous research identifies several personality traits shared by individuals who make effective decisions based on their intuition, such as risk-taking, creativity, flexibility, and emotional intelligence (Burke & Miller, 1999; Matzler et al., 2007). In the recruitment process, managers can use pre-employment tests to identify applicants with these characteristics. Thus, I recommend managers to apply, for instance, the *Employee Personality Profile (EPP)* and *the Criteria Personality Inventory (CPI)* to measure creativity (Criteria, n.d.). Additionally, they can assess the emotional intelligence of candidates by using the *Trait Emotional Intelligence Questionnaire (TEIQue)* in the selection process (O'Connor et al., 2019). By ensuring that individuals are hired who are more likely to use their intuition effectively, managers can encourage effective intuitive decision-making in their organization.

4. Conclusion

The use of intuition in organizational decision-making is becoming increasingly common due to complex, fast-moving, ambiguous, and uncertain work conditions in today's organizations. As a result, manager's decision-making approaches must adapt to the growing intuitive nature of decisions. Intuitive decision-making yields opportunities to improve the decision effectiveness that can benefit organizations. When intuition is used effectively, it leads to creative, innovative, and qualitative outcomes. Furthermore, the use of intuition allows effective decisions to be made under time constraints and in complex situations. To foster effective intuitive decision-making in organizations, managers must consider the characteristics of the decision-maker, the decision task, and the decision environment in their actions. First, they should create an environment that allows for failure, encourages curiosity, and provide opportunities to make new experiences. Moreover, they should improve their employee's decision-making skills by building their expertise through training, mentoring, and feedback. In addition, managers can develop their employee's intuitive awareness by following the suggested guidelines. Finally, managers can enhance the effective use of intuition in their organization by recruiting intuitive individuals based on their personality traits. This paper suggests that managers should acknowledge the presence of intuition in organizational decision-making and take measures to increase its effectiveness to take advantage of its benefits.

13

5. List of references

Ackerman, P. L., & Kanfer, R. (2020). Work in the 21st century: New directions for aging and adult development. *American Psychologist, 75*(4), 486–498.

Albrechtsen, J. S., Meissner, C. A., & Susa, K. J. (2009). Can intuition improve deception detection performance?. *Journal of Experimental Social Psychology, 45*(4), 1052-1055.

Barley, S. R., Bechky, B. A., & Milliken, F. J. (2017). The Changing Nature of Work: Careers, Identities, and Work Lives in the 21st Century. *Academy of Management Discoveries, 3*(2), 111–115.

Burke, L. A., & Miller, M. K. (1999). Taking the mystery out of intuitive decision making. *Academy of Management Perspectives, 13*(4), 91-99.

Ceschi, A., Demerouti, E., Sartori, R., & Weller, J. (2017). Decision-making processes in the workplace: how exhaustion, lack of resources and job demands impair them and affect performance. *Frontiers in Psychology, 8*, 313.

Criteria (n.d.). *Pre-Employment Creativity Tests.* https://www.criteriacorp.com/assessments/measure-creativity

Dane, E., & Pratt, M. G. (2007). Exploring intuition and its role in managerial decision making. *Academy of management review, 32*(1), 33-54.

Dane, E., Rockmann, K. W., & Pratt, M. G. (2012). When should I trust my gut? Linking domain expertise to intuitive decision-making effectiveness. *Organizational Behavior and Human Decision Processes, 119*(2), 187-194.

Dijksterhuis, A., Bos, M. W., Nordgren, L. F., & Van Baaren, R. B. (2006). On making the right choice: The deliberation-without-attention effect. *Science, 311*(5763), 1005-1007.

Elbanna, S. (2006). Strategic decision-making: Process perspectives. *International Journal of Management Reviews, 8*(1), 1-20.

Eubanks, D. L., Murphy, S. T., & Mumford, M. D. (2010). Intuition as an influence on creative problem-solving: The effects of intuition, positive affect, and training. *Creativity Research Journal, 22*(2), 170-184.

Faraji-Rad, A., & Pham, M. T. (2017). Uncertainty increases the reliance on affect in decisions. *Journal of Consumer Research, 44*(1), 1–21.

Garfield, M. J., Taylor, N. J., Dennis, A. R., & Satzinger, J. W. (2001). Research Report: Modifying Paradigms - Individual Differences, Creativity Techniques, and Exposure to Ideas in Group Idea Generation. *Information Systems Research, 12*(3), 322–333.

Halevy, N., & Chou, E. Y. (2014). How decisions happen: Focal points and blind spots in interdependent decision making. *Journal of Personality and Social Psychology, 106*(3), 398–417.

Hodgkinson, G. P., Sadler-Smith, E., Burke, L. A., Claxton, G., & Sparrow, P. R. (2009). Intuition in organizations: Implications for strategic management. *Long Range Planning, 42*(3), 277-297.

Huang, L., & Pearce, J. L. (2015). Managing the unknowable: The effectiveness of early-stage investor gut feel in entrepreneurial investment decisions. *Administrative Science Quarterly, 60*(4), 634-670.

Inbar, Y., Cone, J., & Gilovich, T. (2010). People's intuitions about intuitive insight and intuitive choice. *Journal of Personality and Social Psychology, 99*(2), 232-247.

Kahneman, D., & Klein, G. (2009). Conditions for intuitive expertise: a failure to disagree. *American Psychologist, 64*(6), 515-526.

Khatri, N., & Ng, H. A. (2000). The role of intuition in strategic decision making. *Human Relations, 53*(1), 57-86.

Maier, S. (2017, November 3). *What Google, Adobe, and Cargill Changed About Their Performance Management Strategies.* HR Daily Advisor. *https://hrdailyadvisor.blr.com/2017/11/03/google-adobe-cargill-changed-performance-management-strategies/*

Matzler, K., Bailom, F., & Mooradian, T. A. (2007). Intuitive decision making. *MIT Sloan Management Review, 49*(1), 13-15.

Mick, B. (2014, February 11). *Intuition and Decisions.* Workforce. https://www.workforce.com/uk/news/intuition-and-decisions

Miller, C., C., & Ireland, R. D. (2005). Intuition in Strategic Decision Making: Friend or Foe in the Fast-Paced 21st Century? *The Academy of Management Executive, 19*(1), 19-30.

Nyatanga, B., & Vocht, H. D. (2008). Intuition in clinical decision-making: a psychological penumbra. *International Journal of Palliative Nursing, 14*(10), 492-496.

O'Connor, P. J., Hill, A., Kaya, M., & Martin, B. (2019). The measurement of emotional intelligence: A critical review of the literature and recommendations for researchers and practitioners. *Frontiers in Psychology, 10*, 1116.

Park, J., & Song, J. (2020). How Is Intuitive Thinking Shared and Elaborated During Small-Group Problem-Solving Activities on Thermal Phenomena? *Research in Science Education, 50*, 2363-2390.

Robbins, S. P., & Judge, T. A. (2019). *Organizational Behavior.* Pearson.

Sadler-Smith, E., & Shefy, E. (2004). The intuitive executive: Understanding and applying "gut feel" in decision-making. *Academy of Management Executive, 18*(4), 76–91.

Sadler-Smith, E., & Shefy, E. (2007). Developing intuitive awareness in management education. *Academy of Management Learning & Education, 6*(2), 186-205.

Salas, E., Rosen, M. A., & DiazGranados, D. (2010). Expertise-Based Intuition and Decision Making in Organizations. *Journal of Management, 36*(4), 941-973.

Sauter, V. L. (1999). Intuitive decision-making. *Communications of the ACM, 42*(6), 109-115.

Sinclair, M., & Ashkanasy, N. M. (2005). Intuition: Myth or a Decision-making tool? *Management Learning, 36*(3), 353-370.

Tesolin, A. (2018, August 14). *5 Ways to Use Intuition In Your Training Sessions*. Intuita. https://intuita.com/5-ways-to-use-intuition-in-your-training-session/

Tichá, I., Hron, J., & Fieder, J. (2010). Managerial decision making-importance of intuition in the rational process. *Agricultural Economics*, *56*(12), 553-557.

Usher, M., Russo, Z., Weyers, M., Brauner, R., & Zakay, D. (2011). The impact of the mode of thought in complex decisions: Intuitive decisions are better. *Frontiers in Psychology*, *2*, 37.

Zhu, Y., Ritter, S. M., Müller, B. C. N., & Dijksterhuis, A. (2017). Creativity: Intuitive processing outperforms deliberative processing in creative idea selection. *Journal of Experimental Social Psychology*, *73*, 180–188.

YOUR KNOWLEDGE HAS VALUE

- We will publish your bachelor's and
  master's thesis, essays and papers

- Your own eBook and book -
  sold worldwide in all relevant shops

- Earn money with each sale

Upload your text at www.GRIN.com
and publish for free